Prayer Journal FOR Busy WOMEN

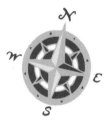

Growing in your relationship with God

By Susan Ayshe Lund

This convenient, easy-to-use prayer journal is dedicated
to you, the reader and writer. As you journal your prayers,
may you experience personal and spiritual growth along
with the inward joy that comes from knowing and
trusting God each and every day.

Published by Learning By Design
P.O. Box 44926, Eden Prairie, MN 55346
ISBN 0-9676629-0-7

Book design: KMF Design
Printed in Canada

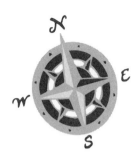

Congratulations!

You have taken the first step toward strengthening the most important relationship in your lifetime — the only relationship that you will have for a lifetime — your relationship with God.

This prayer journal is a convenient, easy-to-use guide for personal growth and practical application. It is designed to help you enrich your faith and embrace the awesome glory of God. Simply devote 10 minutes each day to journal your daily walk with God. In doing so, you will experience tremendous rewards and lasting blessings.

Journaling helps you:

- develop the spiritual discipline required to grow in your relationship with God.
- create spiritual vitality — recognizing God's presence in your daily life, staying in constant contact with God, seeking his guidance and direction in your daily life, and observing how God's plan for your life unfolds.
- experience the inward joy of knowing and trusting God in all situations.
- express gratitude and count your blessings.
- confess your sins and seek forgiveness.
- write out prayer requests for loved ones and those in need.
- glorify God in all you say and do.
- ask him to use you as an instrument to glorify him.
- make a difference in the lives of others.

Who can benefit from journaling?

Busy women, grandmothers, mothers, daughters, sisters, friends, those who work outside the home, traveling professionals — anyone who is willing to commit just 10 minutes a day to pray and recognize God's awesome power and presence. While this was initially designed for busy women, there are no limits to its applications:

Personal use: Journal for your own personal growth and practical application.

Women's Bible study groups: Journal in conjunction with your study guide to reflect on how God is working in your daily life and how you are responding to his guidance. Journal collectively within a study group. Journal for one week, then pass it on to individual group members. When journaling is complete, return to group leader and discuss ways in which God's presence has touched the lives of each participant.

Learn and pass it on: Share your personal story of how journaling strengthened your relationship with God. To be eligible for publication in our next edition, send your story to: Learning By Design, P.O. Box 44926 Eden Prairie, MN 55346.

Guidelines for journaling

Monthly Goals, Review and Reflection

Goals: As you set monthly spiritual goals, you may find it helpful to sit silently for five to 10 minutes and ask God to reveal — in words and images — what he believes you need to work on during the next month. Observe how he speaks to you, and how you hear him.

Review and Reflection: At the end of each month, review your journal entries and reflect on God's guidance in your daily life. Take a red pen and record how and when God answered your prayers. When you need a reminder of God's love, review past blessings. Then turn to the scriptures and notice how unchanging his love is. As you reflect on your monthly goals and daily entries, answer the following questions:

- Are there key themes and patterns emerging?
- What are your prayer habits — frequency, posture, time of day, length of time, etc.?
- Is there anything you want to improve upon?
- What obstacles prevented you from journaling daily?
- How can you overcome these obstacles?
- How did God bless you this month?
- How did you glorify God this month?
- What did you learn from your prayers and responses from God?
- What adjustments can you make in your life as a result of what you learned?
- How have you grown in your faith from journaling this month?

Daily Reflections

What did you do to grow in your relationship with God today? There are many ways to nourish yourself spiritually — reading the Bible, praying, listening to praise and worship music, journaling and serving others. Every day, commit to activities that help you grow in your relationship with God.

How did God bless you today? Praising God takes the focus off yourself and helps you see that, regardless of the circumstances of the day, God is with you and blesses you in amazing ways. Find something to praise God for each day. When you do, you will find your heart elevated from daily distractions to lasting confidence.

What sins did you commit today? Every day, Satan tries to distract you and shift your focus away from God. These distractions can include things like busyness, self-centeredness, jealousy and greed. It is important to make prayer a priority — to ask God for help in defeating Satan's strongholds; to ask God for forgiveness.

Who needs your prayers today? Prayer requests provide an opportunity to focus on the needs of others. When you pray, be specific. Prayer requests can be categorized into four areas: personal, family & friends, community and worldwide. God hears and answers every prayer. Observe how he blesses you and those you pray for.

What did you learn from your journaling today? Journaling, praying and reading the Bible enhance your awareness of God's presence and guidance in your life. Daily commitment to these activities strengthens your understanding of God's time line and his will for you. Make note of these insights.

What adjustments can you make as a result of what you learned today? A Christian life is a changed life. *Listening* is absorbing and accepting the information you read and hear about God. *Learning* is understanding its meaning and implications. *Obeying* is putting into action all you have learned and understood. All three parts are essential to a growing relationship with God.

Praying

Take time to write out your prayers daily. Set aside 10 minutes every day. Begin your day by journaling, praying and reading God's word.

How to pray. Prayer is your personal conversation with God. Be open and honest with yourself and God. When you pray, focus on his presence rather than on how you are expressing yourself. He knows your heart's desires and your every need. If you ask him, he will guide you. As you grow in your relationship with God, your prayer life will mature.

Consistent communication is the foundation of all relationships. The secret of a close relationship with God is to pray to him earnestly every day. Regular communication is fundamental to any friendship and certainly necessary for a strong relationship with God.

Daily reflections S A M P L E

TODAY IS: _November 6, 1999_   **S M T W TH F (S)**

What did I do to grow in my relationship with God today?

   ☑ Read the Bible   ☑ Shared my faith
   ☑ Prayed alone   ☑ Prayed with a friend, family member, spouse
   ○ Served others   ☑ Wrote in my prayer journal
   ○ Listened to Christian music

How did God bless me today?   _• Guided me as I journaled._

• Provided me with spiritual discipline to read the word and journal this morning.

• Blessed me for sharing my faith with a friend.

• Gave me the discipline to improve my health by eating better and exercising.

• Gave me the gift of peace and relaxation.

What sins did I commit today? (List your confessions and seek forgiveness) _Lord, reveal to me any sin that may block my relationship with you._

Forgive me and keep me from deliberate wrongs. Lord, I pray that you fill my heart
with your Holy Spirit.

Who needs my prayers today? _• Guide my little sister as she makes her way_

through college.   _• I pray for spiritual revival within each and every family member_
that you, Lord, transform their hearts so they desire to know you better.
• Lord, align my desires with your purposes. Transform my heart's desire to align
with your will, Lord.   _• Lord, guide me to provide encouragement for my family;_
to lift them up to you in times of trial.

What did I learn today? _Writing out my prayers helps me to focus my thoughts_
on you, Lord. Doing so increases my awareness of your presence in my daily life.

What adjustments can I make in my life as a result of what I learned today? _I can start my day by praying for the spiritual discipline to read_
the word and pray daily.

Prayers

Lord, thank you for this day and all of the many blessings you have given me. I pray that you watch over my husband, family and me today. Guide us spiritually, emotionally and physically, Lord. I pray that Satan's efforts to enter our thoughts, words or actions be cast at the foot of the cross, covered with the blood of the Lamb and rendered powerless in the name of Jesus Christ our Lord. Fill our hearts with your love, peace, wisdom and will, Lord. Help us look to you throughout our busy day and seek your wisdom. Help us find quiet time to listen to your guidance and feel your presence in every situation and conversation. Lord, use us as instruments to glorify you in all that we do, say and think today. In Jesus name I pray, Amen.

Almighty King, little did I know four years ago, when you planted the seed within me to begin a prayer journal, that you would use this as a tool to strengthen my relationship with you. Furthermore, I had no idea this prayer journal would be used to encourage other women to grow in their relationship with you. Lord, I pray that every woman who uses this journal may discover the inward joy of strengthening her relationship with you. Whether she is a baby Christian or a mature Christian, may she become aware of your constant presence and guidance in her daily life. May she become keenly aware of your voice as you speak to her. Give her the spiritual discipline to journal daily and transform her heart's desire to know you like never before. Amen.

Search my heart, Lord, and reveal to me whatever I need to work on. Protect me from sin and keep me from deliberate wrongs. Transform my heart to your desire. Give me the discipline and desire to serve you faithfully. In Jesus name I pray, Amen.

The power of prayer

The Lord is near to all who call on him, to all who
call on him in truth.
Matthew 6:6

Be still and know that I am God.
Psalm 46:10

Rejoice always, pray without ceasing, in everything give thanks;
for this is the will of God in Christ Jesus for you.
1 Thessalonians 5:16-18

"I will do whatever you ask in my name,
so that the Son may bring glory to the Father. You may ask me
for anything in my name, and I will do it," answered Jesus.
John 14: 13-14

If my people, who are called by my name, will humble
themselves and pray and seek my face and turn from their
wicked ways, then I will hear them from heaven and
will forgive their sins and will heal their land.
2 Chronicles 7:14

I wait for you, O Lord; you will answer, O Lord my God.
Psalm 38:15

Very early in the morning, while it was still dark, Jesus got up,
left the house and went off to a solitary place, where he prayed.
Mark 1:35

Do not be anxious about anything, but in everything, by prayer
and petition, with thanksgiving, present your request to God.
And the peace of God, which transcends all understanding,
will guard your hearts and your minds in Christ Jesus.

Philippians 4:6-7

This is the confidence we have in approaching God:
that if we ask anything according to his will, he hears us.
And if we know that he hears us – whatever we ask – we know
that we have what we asked of him.

1 John 5:14-15

For the eyes of the Lord are on the righteous and his ears
are attentive to their prayer.

1 Peter 3:12

Evening and morning and at noon I will pray, and cry aloud,
And he shall hear my voice.

Psalm 55:17

To defend ourselves against the lies and propaganda of our
enemies, our best preparation is to be saturated with the
knowledge of God and filled with his presence. Our daily study
of his word, our prayers, our worship, and confidence in his
presence will keep us strong.

Psalm 6:8-10

If we confess our sins, he is faithful and just and will forgive us
our sins and purify us from all unrighteousness.

1 John 1:9

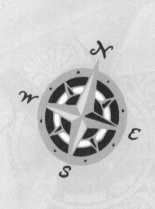

Spiritual goals
for the month of:

What are my three spiritual goals for this month?

1. _____

2. _____

3. _____

Why do I want to achieve these goals?

1. _____

2. _____

3. _____

What obstacles do I anticipate? _____

_____

_____

How will I overcome these obstacles? What support do I need?
(prayer, Bible study, a spiritual director, a Christian friend, etc.)

_____

_____

_____

_____

How will achieving these goals help me to glorify God?_____

_____

_____

_____

Daily reflections

TODAY IS: _____   **S M T W TH F S**

What did I do to grow in my relationship with God today?
- ○ Read the Bible
- ○ Prayed alone
- ○ Served others
- ○ Listened to Christian music
- ○ Shared my faith
- ○ Prayed with a friend, family member, spouse
- ○ Wrote in my prayer journal

How did God bless me today? _____

_____

_____

_____

_____

What sins did I commit today? (List your confessions and seek forgiveness) _____

_____

_____

Who needs my prayers today? _____

_____

_____

_____

_____

What did I learn today?_____

_____

_____

_____

What adjustments can I make in my life as a result of what I learned today?_____

_____

_____

_____

Daily reflections

TODAY IS: _____   **S M T W TH F S**

What did I do to grow in my relationship with God today?
- ○ Read the Bible   ○ Shared my faith
- ○ Prayed alone   ○ Prayed with a friend, family member, spouse
- ○ Served others   ○ Wrote in my prayer journal
- ○ Listened to Christian music

How did God bless me today? _____

_____

_____

_____

_____

What sins did I commit today? (List your confessions and seek forgiveness) _____

_____

_____

Who needs my prayers today? _____

_____

_____

_____

_____

_____

What did I learn today? _____

_____

_____

_____

What adjustments can I make in my life as a result of what I learned today? _____

_____

_____

_____

Daily reflections

TODAY IS: _____   **S M T W TH F S**

What did I do to grow in my relationship with God today?

- ○ Read the Bible
- ○ Shared my faith
- ○ Prayed alone
- ○ Prayed with a friend, family member, spouse
- ○ Served others
- ○ Wrote in my prayer journal
- ○ Listened to Christian music

How did God bless me today? _____

_____

_____

_____

_____

What sins did I commit today? (List your confessions and seek forgiveness) _____

_____

_____

Who needs my prayers today? _____

_____

_____

_____

_____

_____

What did I learn today? _____

_____

_____

_____

What adjustments can I make in my life as a result of what I learned today? _____

_____

_____

_____

Prayers

Daily reflections

TODAY IS: _____   **S M T W TH F S**

What did I do to grow in my relationship with God today?
- ○ Read the Bible
- ○ Shared my faith
- ○ Prayed alone
- ○ Prayed with a friend, family member, spouse
- ○ Served others
- ○ Wrote in my prayer journal
- ○ Listened to Christian music

How did God bless me today? _____

_____

_____

_____

_____

What sins did I commit today? (List your confessions and seek forgiveness) _____

_____

_____

Who needs my prayers today? _____

_____

_____

_____

_____

_____

What did I learn today? _____

_____

_____

_____

What adjustments can I make in my life as a result of what I learned today? _____

_____

_____

_____

Prayers

Daily reflections

TODAY IS: _____   S M T W TH F S

What did I do to grow in my relationship with God today?
- ○ Read the Bible
- ○ Prayed alone
- ○ Served others
- ○ Listened to Christian music
- ○ Shared my faith
- ○ Prayed with a friend, family member, spouse
- ○ Wrote in my prayer journal

How did God bless me today? _____

_____

_____

_____

_____

What sins did I commit today? (List your confessions and seek forgiveness) _____

_____

_____

Who needs my prayers today? _____

_____

_____

_____

_____

_____

What did I learn today? _____

_____

_____

_____

What adjustments can I make in my life as a result of what I learned today? _____

_____

_____

_____

Prayers

Daily reflections

TODAY IS: _____   **S M T W TH F S**

What did I do to grow in my relationship with God today?
- ◯ Read the Bible
- ◯ Shared my faith
- ◯ Prayed alone
- ◯ Prayed with a friend, family member, spouse
- ◯ Served others
- ◯ Wrote in my prayer journal
- ◯ Listened to Christian music

How did God bless me today? _____

_____

_____

_____

_____

What sins did I commit today? (List your confessions and seek forgiveness) _____

_____

_____

Who needs my prayers today? _____

_____

_____

_____

_____

_____

What did I learn today? _____

_____

_____

_____

What adjustments can I make in my life as a result of what I learned today? _____

_____

_____

_____

Prayers

Daily reflections

TODAY IS: _____   **S M T W TH F S**

What did I do to grow in my relationship with God today?

○ Read the Bible   ○ Shared my faith

○ Prayed alone   ○ Prayed with a friend, family member, spouse

○ Served others   ○ Wrote in my prayer journal

○ Listened to Christian music

How did God bless me today? _____

_____

_____

_____

_____

What sins did I commit today? (List your confessions and seek forgiveness) _____

_____

_____

Who needs my prayers today? _____

_____

_____

_____

_____

_____

What did I learn today? _____

_____

_____

_____

What adjustments can I make in my life as a result of what I learned today? _____

_____

_____

_____

Prayers

Daily reflections

TODAY IS: _____   **S M T W TH F S**

What did I do to grow in my relationship with God today?
- ◯ Read the Bible
- ◯ Shared my faith
- ◯ Prayed alone
- ◯ Prayed with a friend, family member, spouse
- ◯ Served others
- ◯ Wrote in my prayer journal
- ◯ Listened to Christian music

How did God bless me today? _____

_____

_____

_____

_____

What sins did I commit today? (List your confessions and seek forgiveness) _____

_____

_____

Who needs my prayers today? _____

_____

_____

_____

_____

_____

What did I learn today? _____

_____

_____

_____

What adjustments can I make in my life as a result of what I learned today? _____

_____

_____

_____

Prayers

Daily reflections

TODAY IS: _____ **S M T W TH F S**

What did I do to grow in my relationship with God today?
- ○ Read the Bible
- ○ Prayed alone
- ○ Served others
- ○ Listened to Christian music
- ○ Shared my faith
- ○ Prayed with a friend, family member, spouse
- ○ Wrote in my prayer journal

How did God bless me today? _____

_____

_____

_____

_____

What sins did I commit today? (List your confessions and seek forgiveness) _____

_____

_____

Who needs my prayers today? _____

_____

_____

_____

_____

_____

What did I learn today? _____

_____

_____

_____

What adjustments can I make in my life as a result of what I learned today? _____

_____

_____

_____

Daily reflections

TODAY IS: _____   **S M T W TH F S**

What did I do to grow in my relationship with God today?
- ◯ Read the Bible
- ◯ Shared my faith
- ◯ Prayed alone
- ◯ Prayed with a friend, family member, spouse
- ◯ Served others
- ◯ Wrote in my prayer journal
- ◯ Listened to Christian music

How did God bless me today? _____

_____

_____

_____

_____

What sins did I commit today? (List your confessions and seek forgiveness) _____

_____

_____

Who needs my prayers today? _____

_____

_____

_____

_____

_____

What did I learn today? _____

_____

_____

_____

What adjustments can I make in my life as a result of what I learned today? _____

_____

_____

_____

Daily reflections

TODAY IS: _____   **S M T W TH F S**

What did I do to grow in my relationship with God today?
- ○ Read the Bible   ○ Shared my faith
- ○ Prayed alone   ○ Prayed with a friend, family member, spouse
- ○ Served others   ○ Wrote in my prayer journal
- ○ Listened to Christian music

How did God bless me today? _____

_____

_____

_____

_____

What sins did I commit today? (List your confessions and seek forgiveness) _____

_____

_____

Who needs my prayers today? _____

_____

_____

_____

_____

_____

What did I learn today? _____

_____

_____

_____

What adjustments can I make in my life as a result of what I learned today? _____

_____

_____

_____

Prayers

Daily reflections

TODAY IS: _____   **S M T W TH F S**

What did I do to grow in my relationship with God today?

○ Read the Bible   ○ Shared my faith
○ Prayed alone   ○ Prayed with a friend, family member, spouse
○ Served others   ○ Wrote in my prayer journal
○ Listened to Christian music

How did God bless me today? _____

_____

_____

_____

_____

What sins did I commit today? (List your confessions and seek forgiveness) _____

_____

_____

Who needs my prayers today? _____

_____

_____

_____

_____

_____

What did I learn today? _____

_____

_____

_____

What adjustments can I make in my life as a result of what I learned today? _____

_____

_____

_____

Prayers

Daily reflections

TODAY IS: _____   **S   M   T   W   TH   F   S**

What did I do to grow in my relationship with God today?
- ○ Read the Bible   ○ Shared my faith
- ○ Prayed alone   ○ Prayed with a friend, family member, spouse
- ○ Served others   ○ Wrote in my prayer journal
- ○ Listened to Christian music

How did God bless me today? _____

_____

_____

_____

_____

What sins did I commit today? (List your confessions and seek forgiveness) _____

_____

_____

Who needs my prayers today? _____

_____

_____

_____

_____

_____

What did I learn today? _____

_____

_____

_____

What adjustments can I make in my life as a result of what I learned today? _____

_____

_____

_____

Prayers

Daily reflections

TODAY IS: _____   **S M T W TH F S**

What did I do to grow in my relationship with God today?
- ○ Read the Bible
- ○ Shared my faith
- ○ Prayed alone
- ○ Prayed with a friend, family member, spouse
- ○ Served others
- ○ Wrote in my prayer journal
- ○ Listened to Christian music

How did God bless me today? _____

_____

_____

_____

_____

What sins did I commit today? (List your confessions and seek forgiveness) _____

_____

_____

Who needs my prayers today? _____

_____

_____

_____

_____

_____

What did I learn today? _____

_____

_____

_____

What adjustments can I make in my life as a result of what I learned today? _____

_____

_____

_____

Prayers

Daily reflections

TODAY IS: _____ **S M T W TH F S**

What did I do to grow in my relationship with God today?
- ○ Read the Bible   ○ Shared my faith
- ○ Prayed alone   ○ Prayed with a friend, family member, spouse
- ○ Served others   ○ Wrote in my prayer journal
- ○ Listened to Christian music

How did God bless me today? _____

_____

_____

_____

_____

What sins did I commit today? (List your confessions and seek forgiveness) _____

_____

_____

Who needs my prayers today? _____

_____

_____

_____

_____

_____

What did I learn today? _____

_____

_____

_____

What adjustments can I make in my life as a result of what I learned today? _____

_____

_____

_____

Prayers

Daily reflections

TODAY IS: _____ **S M T W TH F S**

What did I do to grow in my relationship with God today?
- ○ Read the Bible   ○ Shared my faith
- ○ Prayed alone   ○ Prayed with a friend, family member, spouse
- ○ Served others   ○ Wrote in my prayer journal
- ○ Listened to Christian music

How did God bless me today? _____

_____

_____

_____

_____

What sins did I commit today? (List your confessions and seek forgiveness) _____

_____

_____

Who needs my prayers today? _____

_____

_____

_____

_____

_____

What did I learn today? _____

_____

_____

_____

What adjustments can I make in my life as a result of what I learned today? _____

_____

_____

_____

Daily reflections

TODAY IS: _____   **S M T W TH F S**

What did I do to grow in my relationship with God today?
- ○ Read the Bible
- ○ Shared my faith
- ○ Prayed alone
- ○ Prayed with a friend, family member, spouse
- ○ Served others
- ○ Wrote in my prayer journal
- ○ Listened to Christian music

How did God bless me today? _____

_____

_____

_____

_____

What sins did I commit today? (List your confessions and seek forgiveness) _____

_____

_____

Who needs my prayers today? _____

_____

_____

_____

_____

_____

What did I learn today? _____

_____

_____

_____

What adjustments can I make in my life as a result of what I learned today? _____

_____

_____

_____

Prayers

Daily reflections

TODAY IS: _____   **S   M   T   W   TH   F   S**

What did I do to grow in my relationship with God today?

- ○ Read the Bible   ○ Shared my faith
- ○ Prayed alone   ○ Prayed with a friend, family member, spouse
- ○ Served others   ○ Wrote in my prayer journal
- ○ Listened to Christian music

How did God bless me today? _____

_____

_____

_____

_____

What sins did I commit today? (List your confessions and seek forgiveness) _____

_____

_____

Who needs my prayers today? _____

_____

_____

_____

_____

_____

What did I learn today? _____

_____

_____

_____

What adjustments can I make in my life as a result of what I learned today? _____

_____

_____

_____

Prayers

Daily reflections

TODAY IS: _____   **S M T W TH F S**

What did I do to grow in my relationship with God today?
- ○ Read the Bible
- ○ Shared my faith
- ○ Prayed alone
- ○ Prayed with a friend, family member, spouse
- ○ Served others
- ○ Wrote in my prayer journal
- ○ Listened to Christian music

How did God bless me today? _____

_____

_____

_____

_____

What sins did I commit today? (List your confessions and seek forgiveness) _____

_____

_____

Who needs my prayers today? _____

_____

_____

_____

_____

_____

What did I learn today?_____

_____

_____

_____

What adjustments can I make in my life as a result of what I learned today?_____

_____

_____

_____

Prayers

Daily reflections

TODAY IS: _____   **S M T W TH F S**

What did I do to grow in my relationship with God today?
- ◯ Read the Bible   ◯ Shared my faith
- ◯ Prayed alone   ◯ Prayed with a friend, family member, spouse
- ◯ Served others   ◯ Wrote in my prayer journal
- ◯ Listened to Christian music

How did God bless me today? _____

_____

_____

_____

_____

What sins did I commit today? (List your confessions and seek forgiveness) _____

_____

_____

Who needs my prayers today? _____

_____

_____

_____

_____

_____

What did I learn today? _____

_____

_____

What adjustments can I make in my life as a result of what I learned today? _____

_____

_____

Daily reflections

TODAY IS: _____ **S M T W TH F S**

What did I do to grow in my relationship with God today?
- ○ Read the Bible
- ○ Shared my faith
- ○ Prayed alone
- ○ Prayed with a friend, family member, spouse
- ○ Served others
- ○ Wrote in my prayer journal
- ○ Listened to Christian music

How did God bless me today? _____

_____

_____

_____

_____

What sins did I commit today? (List your confessions and seek forgiveness) _____

_____

_____

Who needs my prayers today? _____

_____

_____

_____

_____

_____

What did I learn today? _____

_____

_____

_____

What adjustments can I make in my life as a result of what I learned today? _____

_____

_____

_____

Prayers

Daily reflections

TODAY IS: _____ **S M T W TH F S**

What did I do to grow in my relationship with God today?
- ○ Read the Bible
- ○ Prayed alone
- ○ Served others
- ○ Listened to Christian music
- ○ Shared my faith
- ○ Prayed with a friend, family member, spouse
- ○ Wrote in my prayer journal

How did God bless me today? _____

_____

_____

_____

_____

What sins did I commit today? (List your confessions and seek forgiveness) _____

_____

_____

Who needs my prayers today? _____

_____

_____

_____

_____

_____

What did I learn today? _____

_____

_____

What adjustments can I make in my life as a result of what I learned today? _____

_____

_____

_____

Daily reflections

TODAY IS: _____   **S M T W TH F S**

What did I do to grow in my relationship with God today?
- ○ Read the Bible
- ○ Prayed alone
- ○ Served others
- ○ Listened to Christian music
- ○ Shared my faith
- ○ Prayed with a friend, family member, spouse
- ○ Wrote in my prayer journal

How did God bless me today? _____

_____

_____

_____

_____

What sins did I commit today? (List your confessions and seek forgiveness) _____

_____

_____

Who needs my prayers today? _____

_____

_____

_____

_____

_____

What did I learn today?_____

_____

_____

_____

What adjustments can I make in my life as a result of what I learned today?_____

_____

_____

_____

Prayers

Daily reflections

TODAY IS: _____   **S M T W TH F S**

What did I do to grow in my relationship with God today?
- ○ Read the Bible
- ○ Prayed alone
- ○ Served others
- ○ Listened to Christian music
- ○ Shared my faith
- ○ Prayed with a friend, family member, spouse
- ○ Wrote in my prayer journal

How did God bless me today? _____

_____

_____

_____

_____

What sins did I commit today? (List your confessions and seek forgiveness) _____

_____

_____

Who needs my prayers today? _____

_____

_____

_____

_____

_____

What did I learn today? _____

_____

_____

_____

What adjustments can I make in my life as a result of what I learned today? _____

_____

_____

_____

Prayers

Daily reflections

TODAY IS: _____   **S M T W TH F S**

What did I do to grow in my relationship with God today?
- ○ Read the Bible
- ○ Prayed alone
- ○ Served others
- ○ Listened to Christian music
- ○ Shared my faith
- ○ Prayed with a friend, family member, spouse
- ○ Wrote in my prayer journal

How did God bless me today? _____

_____

_____

_____

_____

What sins did I commit today? (List your confessions and seek forgiveness) _____

_____

_____

Who needs my prayers today? _____

_____

_____

_____

_____

_____

What did I learn today? _____

_____

_____

_____

What adjustments can I make in my life as a result of what I learned today? _____

_____

_____

_____

Prayers

Daily reflections

TODAY IS: _____   **S M T W TH F S**

What did I do to grow in my relationship with God today?

    ○ Read the Bible   ○ Shared my faith

    ○ Prayed alone   ○ Prayed with a friend, family member, spouse

    ○ Served others   ○ Wrote in my prayer journal

    ○ Listened to Christian music

How did God bless me today? _____

_____

_____

_____

_____

What sins did I commit today? (List your confessions and seek forgiveness) _____

_____

_____

Who needs my prayers today? _____

_____

_____

_____

_____

What did I learn today? _____

_____

_____

What adjustments can I make in my life as a result of what I learned today? _____

_____

_____

Prayers

Daily reflections

TODAY IS: _____   **S M T W TH F S**

What did I do to grow in my relationship with God today?
- ○ Read the Bible
- ○ Shared my faith
- ○ Prayed alone
- ○ Prayed with a friend, family member, spouse
- ○ Served others
- ○ Wrote in my prayer journal
- ○ Listened to Christian music

How did God bless me today? _____

_____

_____

_____

_____

What sins did I commit today? (List your confessions and seek forgiveness) _____

_____

_____

Who needs my prayers today? _____

_____

_____

_____

_____

_____

What did I learn today? _____

_____

_____

_____

What adjustments can I make in my life as a result of what I learned today? _____

_____

_____

_____

Prayers

Daily reflections

TODAY IS: _____   **S M T W TH F S**

What did I do to grow in my relationship with God today?

- ○ Read the Bible
- ○ Prayed alone
- ○ Served others
- ○ Listened to Christian music
- ○ Shared my faith
- ○ Prayed with a friend, family member, spouse
- ○ Wrote in my prayer journal

How did God bless me today? _____

_____

_____

_____

_____

What sins did I commit today? (List your confessions and seek forgiveness) _____

_____

_____

Who needs my prayers today? _____

_____

_____

_____

_____

What did I learn today? _____

_____

_____

_____

What adjustments can I make in my life as a result of what I learned today? _____

_____

_____

_____

Daily reflections

TODAY IS: _____ **S M T W TH F S**

What did I do to grow in my relationship with God today?
- ○ Read the Bible
- ○ Prayed alone
- ○ Served others
- ○ Listened to Christian music
- ○ Shared my faith
- ○ Prayed with a friend, family member, spouse
- ○ Wrote in my prayer journal

How did God bless me today? _____

_____

_____

_____

_____

What sins did I commit today? (List your confessions and seek forgiveness) _____

_____

_____

Who needs my prayers today? _____

_____

_____

_____

_____

_____

What did I learn today? _____

_____

_____

What adjustments can I make in my life as a result of what I learned today? _____

_____

_____

_____

Daily reflections

TODAY IS: _____   **S M T W TH   F S**

What did I do to grow in my relationship with God today?
- ○ Read the Bible   ○ Shared my faith
- ○ Prayed alone   ○ Prayed with a friend, family member, spouse
- ○ Served others   ○ Wrote in my prayer journal
- ○ Listened to Christian music

How did God bless me today? _____

_____

_____

_____

_____

What sins did I commit today? (List your confessions and seek forgiveness) _____

_____

_____

Who needs my prayers today? _____

_____

_____

_____

_____

_____

What did I learn today? _____

_____

_____

_____

What adjustments can I make in my life as a result of what I learned today? _____

_____

_____

_____

Prayers

Daily reflections

TODAY IS: _____   **S M T W TH F S**

What did I do to grow in my relationship with God today?
- ○ Read the Bible   ○ Shared my faith
- ○ Prayed alone   ○ Prayed with a friend, family member, spouse
- ○ Served others   ○ Wrote in my prayer journal
- ○ Listened to Christian music

How did God bless me today? _____

_____

_____

_____

_____

What sins did I commit today? (List your confessions and seek forgiveness) _____

_____

_____

Who needs my prayers today? _____

_____

_____

_____

_____

_____

What did I learn today?_____

_____

_____

_____

What adjustments can I make in my life as a result of what I learned today?_____

_____

_____

_____

Prayers

Month in review

What specific actions did I take toward meeting my goals?

1. _____

2. _____

3. _____

What did I learn this month? (How did God guide me? How did he use me as an instrument to glorify him?)

_____

_____

_____

_____

_____

_____

_____

_____

_____

_____

What adjustments can I make in my life as a result of what I learned this month?

_____

_____

_____

_____

_____

Spiritual goals
for the month of:

What are my three spiritual goals for this month?

1. _____
2. _____
3. _____

Why do I want to achieve these goals?

1. _____
2. _____
3. _____

What obstacles do I anticipate? _____

_____

_____

How will I overcome these obstacles? What support do I need? (prayer, Bible study, a spiritual director, a Christian friend, etc.)

_____

_____

_____

_____

How will achieving these goals help me to glorify God? _____

_____

_____

_____

Daily reflections

TODAY IS: _____   **S M T W TH F S**

What did I do to grow in my relationship with God today?
- ○ Read the Bible   ○ Shared my faith
- ○ Prayed alone   ○ Prayed with a friend, family member, spouse
- ○ Served others   ○ Wrote in my prayer journal
- ○ Listened to Christian music

How did God bless me today? _____

_____

_____

_____

_____

What sins did I commit today? (List your confessions and seek forgiveness) _____

_____

_____

Who needs my prayers today? _____

_____

_____

_____

_____

_____

What did I learn today? _____

_____

_____

_____

What adjustments can I make in my life as a result of what I learned today? _____

_____

_____

_____

Daily reflections

TODAY IS: _____   **S   M   T   W   TH   F   S**

What did I do to grow in my relationship with God today?
- ○ Read the Bible   ○ Shared my faith
- ○ Prayed alone   ○ Prayed with a friend, family member, spouse
- ○ Served others   ○ Wrote in my prayer journal
- ○ Listened to Christian music

How did God bless me today? _____

_____

_____

_____

_____

What sins did I commit today? (List your confessions and seek forgiveness) _____

_____

_____

Who needs my prayers today? _____

_____

_____

_____

_____

_____

What did I learn today? _____

_____

_____

_____

What adjustments can I make in my life as a result of what I learned today? _____

_____

_____

_____

Prayers

Daily reflections

TODAY IS: _____ **S M T W TH F S**

What did I do to grow in my relationship with God today?
- ○ Read the Bible   ○ Shared my faith
- ○ Prayed alone   ○ Prayed with a friend, family member, spouse
- ○ Served others   ○ Wrote in my prayer journal
- ○ Listened to Christian music

How did God bless me today? _____

_____

_____

_____

_____

What sins did I commit today? (List your confessions and seek forgiveness) _____

_____

_____

Who needs my prayers today? _____

_____

_____

_____

_____

_____

What did I learn today? _____

_____

_____

_____

What adjustments can I make in my life as a result of what I learned today? _____

_____

_____

_____

Daily reflections

TODAY IS: _____   **S M T W TH F S**

What did I do to grow in my relationship with God today?

○ Read the Bible   ○ Shared my faith
○ Prayed alone   ○ Prayed with a friend, family member, spouse
○ Served others   ○ Wrote in my prayer journal
○ Listened to Christian music

How did God bless me today? _____

_____

_____

_____

What sins did I commit today? (List your confessions and seek forgiveness) _____

_____

_____

Who needs my prayers today? _____

_____

_____

_____

_____

What did I learn today? _____

_____

_____

_____

What adjustments can I make in my life as a result of what I learned today? _____

_____

_____

Daily reflections

TODAY IS: _____ **S M T W TH F S**

What did I do to grow in my relationship with God today?
- ○ Read the Bible
- ○ Prayed alone
- ○ Served others
- ○ Listened to Christian music
- ○ Shared my faith
- ○ Prayed with a friend, family member, spouse
- ○ Wrote in my prayer journal

How did God bless me today? _____

_____

_____

_____

_____

What sins did I commit today? (List your confessions and seek forgiveness) _____

_____

_____

Who needs my prayers today? _____

_____

_____

_____

_____

_____

What did I learn today? _____

_____

_____

_____

What adjustments can I make in my life as a result of what I learned today? _____

_____

_____

_____

Daily reflections

TODAY IS: _____ **S M T W TH F S**

What did I do to grow in my relationship with God today?
- ○ Read the Bible
- ○ Prayed alone
- ○ Served others
- ○ Listened to Christian music
- ○ Shared my faith
- ○ Prayed with a friend, family member, spouse
- ○ Wrote in my prayer journal

How did God bless me today? _____

_____

_____

_____

_____

What sins did I commit today? (List your confessions and seek forgiveness) _____

_____

_____

Who needs my prayers today? _____

_____

_____

_____

_____

_____

What did I learn today? _____

_____

_____

_____

What adjustments can I make in my life as a result of what I learned today? _____

_____

_____

_____

Daily reflections

TODAY IS: _____ **S M T W TH F S**

What did I do to grow in my relationship with God today?
- ○ Read the Bible
- ○ Prayed alone
- ○ Served others
- ○ Listened to Christian music
- ○ Shared my faith
- ○ Prayed with a friend, family member, spouse
- ○ Wrote in my prayer journal

How did God bless me today? _____

_____

_____

_____

_____

What sins did I commit today? (List your confessions and seek forgiveness) _____

_____

_____

Who needs my prayers today? _____

_____

_____

_____

_____

_____

What did I learn today? _____

_____

_____

_____

What adjustments can I make in my life as a result of what I learned today? _____

_____

_____

_____

Prayers

Daily reflections

TODAY IS: _____ **S M T W TH F S**

What did I do to grow in my relationship with God today?
- ○ Read the Bible   ○ Shared my faith
- ○ Prayed alone   ○ Prayed with a friend, family member, spouse
- ○ Served others   ○ Wrote in my prayer journal
- ○ Listened to Christian music

How did God bless me today? _____

_____

_____

_____

_____

What sins did I commit today? (List your confessions and seek forgiveness) _____

_____

_____

Who needs my prayers today? _____

_____

_____

_____

_____

_____

What did I learn today? _____

_____

_____

_____

What adjustments can I make in my life as a result of what I learned today? _____

_____

_____

_____

Daily reflections

TODAY IS: _____   **S   M   T   W   TH   F   S**

What did I do to grow in my relationship with God today?
- ○ Read the Bible   ○ Shared my faith
- ○ Prayed alone   ○ Prayed with a friend, family member, spouse
- ○ Served others   ○ Wrote in my prayer journal
- ○ Listened to Christian music

How did God bless me today? _____

_____

_____

_____

_____

What sins did I commit today? (List your confessions and seek forgiveness) _____

_____

_____

Who needs my prayers today? _____

_____

_____

_____

_____

What did I learn today? _____

_____

_____

What adjustments can I make in my life as a result of what I learned today? _____

_____

_____

Daily reflections

TODAY IS: _____   **S M T W TH F S**

What did I do to grow in my relationship with God today?
- ○ Read the Bible
- ○ Prayed alone
- ○ Served others
- ○ Listened to Christian music
- ○ Shared my faith
- ○ Prayed with a friend, family member, spouse
- ○ Wrote in my prayer journal

How did God bless me today? _____

_____

_____

_____

_____

What sins did I commit today? (List your confessions and seek forgiveness) _____

_____

_____

Who needs my prayers today? _____

_____

_____

_____

_____

What did I learn today? _____

_____

_____

_____

What adjustments can I make in my life as a result of what I learned today? _____

_____

_____

_____

Prayers

Daily reflections

TODAY IS: _____   **S M T W TH F S**

What did I do to grow in my relationship with God today?
- ○ Read the Bible
- ○ Shared my faith
- ○ Prayed alone
- ○ Prayed with a friend, family member, spouse
- ○ Served others
- ○ Wrote in my prayer journal
- ○ Listened to Christian music

How did God bless me today? _____

_____

_____

_____

_____

What sins did I commit today? (List your confessions and seek forgiveness) _____

_____

_____

Who needs my prayers today? _____

_____

_____

_____

_____

_____

What did I learn today? _____

_____

_____

_____

What adjustments can I make in my life as a result of what I learned today? _____

_____

_____

_____

Daily reflections

TODAY IS: _____ S M T W TH F S

What did I do to grow in my relationship with God today?
- ○ Read the Bible
- ○ Prayed alone
- ○ Served others
- ○ Listened to Christian music
- ○ Shared my faith
- ○ Prayed with a friend, family member, spouse
- ○ Wrote in my prayer journal

How did God bless me today? _____

_____

_____

_____

_____

What sins did I commit today? (List your confessions and seek forgiveness) _____

_____

_____

Who needs my prayers today? _____

_____

_____

_____

_____

What did I learn today? _____

_____

_____

_____

What adjustments can I make in my life as a result of what I learned today? _____

_____

_____

_____

Prayers

Daily reflections

TODAY IS: _____   **S   M   T   W   TH   F   S**

What did I do to grow in my relationship with God today?
- ○ Read the Bible   ○ Shared my faith
- ○ Prayed alone   ○ Prayed with a friend, family member, spouse
- ○ Served others   ○ Wrote in my prayer journal
- ○ Listened to Christian music

How did God bless me today? _____

_____

_____

_____

_____

What sins did I commit today? (List your confessions and seek forgiveness) _____

_____

_____

Who needs my prayers today? _____

_____

_____

_____

_____

What did I learn today? _____

_____

_____

_____

What adjustments can I make in my life as a result of what I learned today? _____

_____

_____

_____

Prayers

Daily reflections

TODAY IS: _____   **S M T W TH F S**

What did I do to grow in my relationship with God today?
- ○ Read the Bible   ○ Shared my faith
- ○ Prayed alone   ○ Prayed with a friend, family member, spouse
- ○ Served others   ○ Wrote in my prayer journal
- ○ Listened to Christian music

How did God bless me today? _____

_____

_____

_____

_____

What sins did I commit today? (List your confessions and seek forgiveness) _____

_____

_____

Who needs my prayers today? _____

_____

_____

_____

_____

_____

What did I learn today? _____

_____

_____

_____

What adjustments can I make in my life as a result of what I learned today? _____

_____

_____

_____

Prayers

Daily reflections

TODAY IS: _____ **S M T W TH F S**

What did I do to grow in my relationship with God today?
- ○ Read the Bible
- ○ Shared my faith
- ○ Prayed alone
- ○ Prayed with a friend, family member, spouse
- ○ Served others
- ○ Wrote in my prayer journal
- ○ Listened to Christian music

How did God bless me today? _____

_____

_____

_____

_____

What sins did I commit today? (List your confessions and seek forgiveness) _____

_____

_____

Who needs my prayers today? _____

_____

_____

_____

_____

_____

What did I learn today? _____

_____

_____

_____

What adjustments can I make in my life as a result of what I learned today? _____

_____

_____

_____

Prayers

Daily reflections

TODAY IS: _____ **S M T W TH F S**

What did I do to grow in my relationship with God today?
- ○ Read the Bible
- ○ Shared my faith
- ○ Prayed alone
- ○ Prayed with a friend, family member, spouse
- ○ Served others
- ○ Wrote in my prayer journal
- ○ Listened to Christian music

How did God bless me today? _____

_____

_____

_____

_____

What sins did I commit today? (List your confessions and seek forgiveness) _____

_____

_____

Who needs my prayers today? _____

_____

_____

_____

_____

_____

What did I learn today?_____

_____

_____

_____

What adjustments can I make in my life as a result of what I learned today?_____

_____

_____

_____

Prayers

Daily reflections

TODAY IS: _____ **S M T W TH F S**

What did I do to grow in my relationship with God today?

    ○ Read the Bible   ○ Shared my faith

    ○ Prayed alone   ○ Prayed with a friend, family member, spouse

    ○ Served others   ○ Wrote in my prayer journal

    ○ Listened to Christian music

How did God bless me today? _____

_____

_____

_____

_____

What sins did I commit today? (List your confessions and seek forgiveness) _____

_____

_____

Who needs my prayers today? _____

_____

_____

_____

_____

_____

What did I learn today? _____

_____

_____

_____

What adjustments can I make in my life as a result of what I learned today? _____

_____

_____

_____

Daily reflections

TODAY IS: _____ **S M T W TH F S**

What did I do to grow in my relationship with God today?
- ○ Read the Bible
- ○ Prayed alone
- ○ Served others
- ○ Listened to Christian music
- ○ Shared my faith
- ○ Prayed with a friend, family member, spouse
- ○ Wrote in my prayer journal

How did God bless me today? _____

_____

_____

_____

_____

What sins did I commit today? (List your confessions and seek forgiveness) _____

_____

_____

Who needs my prayers today? _____

_____

_____

_____

_____

_____

What did I learn today?_____

_____

_____

_____

What adjustments can I make in my life as a result of what I learned today?_____

_____

_____

_____

Prayers

Daily reflections

TODAY IS: _____ **S M T W TH F S**

What did I do to grow in my relationship with God today?
- ○ Read the Bible
- ○ Prayed alone
- ○ Served others
- ○ Listened to Christian music
- ○ Shared my faith
- ○ Prayed with a friend, family member, spouse
- ○ Wrote in my prayer journal

How did God bless me today? _____

_____

_____

_____

_____

What sins did I commit today? (List your confessions and seek forgiveness) _____

_____

_____

Who needs my prayers today? _____

_____

_____

_____

_____

What did I learn today? _____

_____

_____

What adjustments can I make in my life as a result of what I learned today? _____

_____

_____

_____

Daily reflections

TODAY IS: _____ **S M T W TH F S**

What did I do to grow in my relationship with God today?

○ Read the Bible   ○ Shared my faith
○ Prayed alone   ○ Prayed with a friend, family member, spouse
○ Served others   ○ Wrote in my prayer journal
○ Listened to Christian music

How did God bless me today? _____

_____

_____

_____

_____

What sins did I commit today? (List your confessions and seek forgiveness) _____

_____

_____

Who needs my prayers today? _____

_____

_____

_____

_____

_____

What did I learn today? _____

_____

_____

_____

What adjustments can I make in my life as a result of what I learned today? _____

_____

_____

_____

Daily reflections

TODAY IS: _____   **S   M   T   W   TH   F   S**

What did I do to grow in my relationship with God today?
- ○ Read the Bible   ○ Shared my faith
- ○ Prayed alone   ○ Prayed with a friend, family member, spouse
- ○ Served others   ○ Wrote in my prayer journal
- ○ Listened to Christian music

How did God bless me today? _____

_____

_____

_____

_____

What sins did I commit today? (List your confessions and seek forgiveness) _____

_____

_____

Who needs my prayers today? _____

_____

_____

_____

_____

_____

What did I learn today? _____

_____

_____

_____

What adjustments can I make in my life as a result of what I learned today? _____

_____

_____

_____

Daily reflections

TODAY IS: _____ **S M T W TH F S**

What did I do to grow in my relationship with God today?
- ○ Read the Bible   ○ Shared my faith
- ○ Prayed alone   ○ Prayed with a friend, family member, spouse
- ○ Served others   ○ Wrote in my prayer journal
- ○ Listened to Christian music

How did God bless me today? _____

_____

_____

_____

_____

What sins did I commit today? (List your confessions and seek forgiveness) _____

_____

_____

Who needs my prayers today? _____

_____

_____

_____

_____

What did I learn today? _____

_____

_____

_____

What adjustments can I make in my life as a result of what I learned today? _____

_____

_____

_____

Daily reflections

TODAY IS: _____ **S M T W TH F S**

What did I do to grow in my relationship with God today?
- ○ Read the Bible
- ○ Shared my faith
- ○ Prayed alone
- ○ Prayed with a friend, family member, spouse
- ○ Served others
- ○ Wrote in my prayer journal
- ○ Listened to Christian music

How did God bless me today? _____

_____

_____

_____

_____

What sins did I commit today? (List your confessions and seek forgiveness) _____

_____

_____

Who needs my prayers today? _____

_____

_____

_____

_____

What did I learn today? _____

_____

_____

What adjustments can I make in my life as a result of what I learned today? _____

_____

_____

_____

Prayers

Daily reflections

TODAY IS: _____ **S M T W TH F S**

What did I do to grow in my relationship with God today?
- ○ Read the Bible   ○ Shared my faith
- ○ Prayed alone   ○ Prayed with a friend, family member, spouse
- ○ Served others   ○ Wrote in my prayer journal
- ○ Listened to Christian music

How did God bless me today? _____

_____

_____

_____

What sins did I commit today? (List your confessions and seek forgiveness) _____

_____

_____

Who needs my prayers today? _____

_____

_____

_____

_____

What did I learn today? _____

_____

_____

What adjustments can I make in my life as a result of what I learned today? _____

_____

_____

_____

Prayers

Daily reflections

TODAY IS: _____   **S M T W TH F S**

What did I do to grow in my relationship with God today?
- ○ Read the Bible
- ○ Prayed alone
- ○ Served others
- ○ Listened to Christian music
- ○ Shared my faith
- ○ Prayed with a friend, family member, spouse
- ○ Wrote in my prayer journal

How did God bless me today? _____

_____

_____

_____

_____

What sins did I commit today? (List your confessions and seek forgiveness) _____

_____

_____

Who needs my prayers today? _____

_____

_____

_____

_____

_____

What did I learn today? _____

_____

_____

_____

What adjustments can I make in my life as a result of what I learned today? _____

_____

_____

_____

Daily reflections

TODAY IS: _____   **S M T W TH F S**

What did I do to grow in my relationship with God today?
- ○ Read the Bible
- ○ Shared my faith
- ○ Prayed alone
- ○ Prayed with a friend, family member, spouse
- ○ Served others
- ○ Wrote in my prayer journal
- ○ Listened to Christian music

How did God bless me today? _____

_____

_____

_____

_____

What sins did I commit today? (List your confessions and seek forgiveness) _____

_____

_____

Who needs my prayers today? _____

_____

_____

_____

_____

What did I learn today? _____

_____

_____

_____

What adjustments can I make in my life as a result of what I learned today? _____

_____

_____

_____

Prayers

Daily reflections

TODAY IS: _____ **S M T W TH F S**

What did I do to grow in my relationship with God today?

- ○ Read the Bible
- ○ Prayed alone
- ○ Served others
- ○ Listened to Christian music
- ○ Shared my faith
- ○ Prayed with a friend, family member, spouse
- ○ Wrote in my prayer journal

How did God bless me today? _____

_____

_____

_____

_____

What sins did I commit today? (List your confessions and seek forgiveness) _____

_____

_____

Who needs my prayers today? _____

_____

_____

_____

_____

What did I learn today?_____

_____

_____

_____

What adjustments can I make in my life as a result of what I learned today?_____

_____

_____

_____

Daily reflections

TODAY IS: _____   **S M T W TH F S**

What did I do to grow in my relationship with God today?

- ○ Read the Bible   ○ Shared my faith
- ○ Prayed alone   ○ Prayed with a friend, family member, spouse
- ○ Served others   ○ Wrote in my prayer journal
- ○ Listened to Christian music

How did God bless me today? _____

_____

_____

_____

_____

What sins did I commit today? (List your confessions and seek forgiveness) _____

_____

_____

Who needs my prayers today? _____

_____

_____

_____

_____

_____

What did I learn today? _____

_____

_____

_____

What adjustments can I make in my life as a result of what I learned today? _____

_____

_____

_____

Daily reflections

TODAY IS: _____   **S M T W TH F S**

What did I do to grow in my relationship with God today?
- ○ Read the Bible
- ○ Prayed alone
- ○ Served others
- ○ Listened to Christian music
- ○ Shared my faith
- ○ Prayed with a friend, family member, spouse
- ○ Wrote in my prayer journal

How did God bless me today? _____

_____

_____

_____

_____

What sins did I commit today? (List your confessions and seek forgiveness) _____

_____

_____

Who needs my prayers today? _____

_____

_____

_____

_____

_____

What did I learn today? _____

_____

_____

_____

What adjustments can I make in my life as a result of what I learned today? _____

_____

_____

_____

Prayers

Daily reflections

TODAY IS: _____   **S M T W TH F S**

What did I do to grow in my relationship with God today?
- ○ Read the Bible
- ○ Prayed alone
- ○ Served others
- ○ Listened to Christian music
- ○ Shared my faith
- ○ Prayed with a friend, family member, spouse
- ○ Wrote in my prayer journal

How did God bless me today? _____

_____

_____

_____

_____

What sins did I commit today? (List your confessions and seek forgiveness) _____

_____

_____

Who needs my prayers today? _____

_____

_____

_____

_____

_____

What did I learn today? _____

_____

_____

_____

What adjustments can I make in my life as a result of what I learned today? _____

_____

_____

_____

Prayers

Daily reflections

TODAY IS: _____   **S   M   T   W   TH   F   S**

What did I do to grow in my relationship with God today?
- ○ Read the Bible   ○ Shared my faith
- ○ Prayed alone   ○ Prayed with a friend, family member, spouse
- ○ Served others   ○ Wrote in my prayer journal
- ○ Listened to Christian music

How did God bless me today? _____

_____

_____

_____

_____

What sins did I commit today? (List your confessions and seek forgiveness) _____

_____

_____

Who needs my prayers today? _____

_____

_____

_____

_____

_____

What did I learn today? _____

_____

_____

_____

What adjustments can I make in my life as a result of what I learned today? _____

_____

_____

_____

Prayers

Month in review

What specific actions did I take toward meeting my goals?

1. _____

2. _____

3. _____

What did I learn this month? (How did God guide me? How did he use me as an instrument to glorify him?)

_____

_____

_____

_____

_____

_____

_____

_____

_____

_____

_____

What adjustments can I make in my life as a result of what I learned this month?

_____

_____

_____

_____

_____

_____

Spiritual goals
for the month of:

What are my three spiritual goals for this month?

1. _____

2. _____

3. _____

Why do I want to achieve these goals?

1. _____

2. _____

3. _____

What obstacles do I anticipate? _____

_____

_____

How will I overcome these obstacles? What support do I need?
(prayer, Bible study, a spiritual director, a Christian friend, etc.)

_____

_____

_____

_____

How will achieving these goals help me to glorify God? _____

_____

_____

_____

Daily reflections

TODAY IS: _____ **S M T W TH F S**

What did I do to grow in my relationship with God today?
- ○ Read the Bible
- ○ Prayed alone
- ○ Served others
- ○ Listened to Christian music
- ○ Shared my faith
- ○ Prayed with a friend, family member, spouse
- ○ Wrote in my prayer journal

How did God bless me today? _____

_____

_____

_____

_____

What sins did I commit today? (List your confessions and seek forgiveness) _____

_____

_____

Who needs my prayers today? _____

_____

_____

_____

_____

_____

What did I learn today? _____

_____

_____

_____

What adjustments can I make in my life as a result of what I learned today? _____

_____

_____

_____

Daily reflections

TODAY IS: _____   **S M T W TH F S**

What did I do to grow in my relationship with God today?
- ○ Read the Bible
- ○ Prayed alone
- ○ Served others
- ○ Listened to Christian music
- ○ Shared my faith
- ○ Prayed with a friend, family member, spouse
- ○ Wrote in my prayer journal

How did God bless me today? _____

_____

_____

_____

_____

What sins did I commit today? (List your confessions and seek forgiveness) _____

_____

_____

Who needs my prayers today? _____

_____

_____

_____

_____

What did I learn today? _____

_____

_____

_____

What adjustments can I make in my life as a result of what I learned today? _____

_____

_____

_____

Prayers

Daily reflections

TODAY IS: _____   **S   M   T   W   TH   F   S**

What did I do to grow in my relationship with God today?
- ○ Read the Bible
- ○ Prayed alone
- ○ Served others
- ○ Listened to Christian music
- ○ Shared my faith
- ○ Prayed with a friend, family member, spouse
- ○ Wrote in my prayer journal

How did God bless me today? _____

_____

_____

_____

What sins did I commit today? (List your confessions and seek forgiveness) _____

_____

_____

Who needs my prayers today? _____

_____

_____

_____

_____

What did I learn today? _____

_____

_____

What adjustments can I make in my life as a result of what I learned today? _____

_____

_____

Prayers

Daily reflections

TODAY IS: _____   **S M T W TH F S**

What did I do to grow in my relationship with God today?
- ○ Read the Bible
- ○ Prayed alone
- ○ Served others
- ○ Listened to Christian music
- ○ Shared my faith
- ○ Prayed with a friend, family member, spouse
- ○ Wrote in my prayer journal

How did God bless me today? _____

_____

_____

_____

What sins did I commit today? (List your confessions and seek forgiveness) _____

_____

_____

Who needs my prayers today? _____

_____

_____

_____

_____

What did I learn today? _____

_____

_____

What adjustments can I make in my life as a result of what I learned today? _____

_____

_____

Prayers

Daily reflections

TODAY IS: _____   **S   M   T   W   TH   F   S**

What did I do to grow in my relationship with God today?
- ○ Read the Bible   ○ Shared my faith
- ○ Prayed alone   ○ Prayed with a friend, family member, spouse
- ○ Served others   ○ Wrote in my prayer journal
- ○ Listened to Christian music

How did God bless me today? _____

_____

_____

_____

_____

What sins did I commit today? (List your confessions and seek forgiveness) _____

_____

_____

Who needs my prayers today? _____

_____

_____

_____

_____

_____

What did I learn today?_____

_____

_____

_____

What adjustments can I make in my life as a result of what I learned today?_____

_____

_____

_____

Daily reflections

TODAY IS: _____ **S M T W TH F S**

What did I do to grow in my relationship with God today?

- ◯ Read the Bible
- ◯ Shared my faith
- ◯ Prayed alone
- ◯ Prayed with a friend, family member, spouse
- ◯ Served others
- ◯ Wrote in my prayer journal
- ◯ Listened to Christian music

How did God bless me today? _____

_____

_____

_____

_____

What sins did I commit today? (List your confessions and seek forgiveness) _____

_____

_____

Who needs my prayers today? _____

_____

_____

_____

_____

What did I learn today? _____

_____

_____

_____

What adjustments can I make in my life as a result of what I learned today? _____

_____

_____

_____

Prayers

Daily reflections

TODAY IS: _____ **S M T W TH F S**

What did I do to grow in my relationship with God today?
- ○ Read the Bible
- ○ Shared my faith
- ○ Prayed alone
- ○ Prayed with a friend, family member, spouse
- ○ Served others
- ○ Wrote in my prayer journal
- ○ Listened to Christian music

How did God bless me today? _____

_____

_____

_____

_____

What sins did I commit today? (List your confessions and seek forgiveness) _____

_____

_____

Who needs my prayers today? _____

_____

_____

_____

_____

_____

What did I learn today? _____

_____

_____

_____

What adjustments can I make in my life as a result of what I learned today? _____

_____

_____

_____

Prayers

Daily reflections

TODAY IS: _____ **S M T W TH F S**

What did I do to grow in my relationship with God today?
- ○ Read the Bible
- ○ Shared my faith
- ○ Prayed alone
- ○ Prayed with a friend, family member, spouse
- ○ Served others
- ○ Wrote in my prayer journal
- ○ Listened to Christian music

How did God bless me today? _____

_____

_____

_____

_____

What sins did I commit today? (List your confessions and seek forgiveness) _____

_____

_____

Who needs my prayers today? _____

_____

_____

_____

_____

What did I learn today? _____

_____

_____

What adjustments can I make in my life as a result of what I learned today? _____

_____

_____

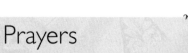

Prayers

Daily reflections

TODAY IS: _____   **S M T W TH F S**

What did I do to grow in my relationship with God today?

    O Read the Bible   O Shared my faith
    O Prayed alone   O Prayed with a friend, family member, spouse
    O Served others   O Wrote in my prayer journal
    O Listened to Christian music

How did God bless me today? _____

_____

_____

_____

_____

What sins did I commit today? (List your confessions and seek forgiveness) _____

_____

_____

Who needs my prayers today? _____

_____

_____

_____

_____

What did I learn today? _____

_____

_____

_____

What adjustments can I make in my life as a result of what I learned today? _____

_____

_____

_____

Daily reflections

TODAY IS: _____ **S M T W TH F S**

What did I do to grow in my relationship with God today?
- ○ Read the Bible
- ○ Prayed alone
- ○ Served others
- ○ Listened to Christian music
- ○ Shared my faith
- ○ Prayed with a friend, family member, spouse
- ○ Wrote in my prayer journal

How did God bless me today? _____

_____

_____

_____

_____

What sins did I commit today? (List your confessions and seek forgiveness) _____

_____

_____

Who needs my prayers today? _____

_____

_____

_____

_____

_____

What did I learn today? _____

_____

_____

_____

What adjustments can I make in my life as a result of what I learned today? _____

_____

_____

_____

Prayers

Daily reflections

TODAY IS: _____ **S M T W TH F S**

What did I do to grow in my relationship with God today?
- ○ Read the Bible
- ○ Shared my faith
- ○ Prayed alone
- ○ Prayed with a friend, family member, spouse
- ○ Served others
- ○ Wrote in my prayer journal
- ○ Listened to Christian music

How did God bless me today? _____

_____

_____

_____

_____

What sins did I commit today? (List your confessions and seek forgiveness) _____

_____

_____

Who needs my prayers today? _____

_____

_____

_____

_____

What did I learn today? _____

_____

_____

What adjustments can I make in my life as a result of what I learned today? _____

_____

_____

Daily reflections

TODAY IS: _____   **S   M   T   W   TH   F   S**

What did I do to grow in my relationship with God today?
- ○ Read the Bible
- ○ Prayed alone
- ○ Served others
- ○ Listened to Christian music
- ○ Shared my faith
- ○ Prayed with a friend, family member, spouse
- ○ Wrote in my prayer journal

How did God bless me today? _____

_____

_____

_____

_____

What sins did I commit today? (List your confessions and seek forgiveness) _____

_____

_____

Who needs my prayers today? _____

_____

_____

_____

_____

_____

What did I learn today? _____

_____

_____

_____

What adjustments can I make in my life as a result of what I learned today? _____

_____

_____

_____

Daily reflections

TODAY IS: _____ **S M T W TH F S**

What did I do to grow in my relationship with God today?
- ○ Read the Bible ○ Shared my faith
- ○ Prayed alone ○ Prayed with a friend, family member, spouse
- ○ Served others ○ Wrote in my prayer journal
- ○ Listened to Christian music

How did God bless me today? _____

_____

_____

_____

_____

What sins did I commit today? (List your confessions and seek forgiveness) _____

_____

_____

Who needs my prayers today? _____

_____

_____

_____

_____

What did I learn today? _____

_____

_____

What adjustments can I make in my life as a result of what I learned today? _____

_____

_____

Prayers

Daily reflections

TODAY IS: _____ **S M T W TH F S**

What did I do to grow in my relationship with God today?

○ Read the Bible   ○ Shared my faith
○ Prayed alone   ○ Prayed with a friend, family member, spouse
○ Served others   ○ Wrote in my prayer journal
○ Listened to Christian music

How did God bless me today? _____

_____

_____

_____

_____

What sins did I commit today? (List your confessions and seek forgiveness) _____

_____

_____

Who needs my prayers today? _____

_____

_____

_____

_____

_____

What did I learn today? _____

_____

_____

_____

What adjustments can I make in my life as a result of what I learned today? _____

_____

_____

_____

Prayers

Daily reflections

TODAY IS: _____ **S M T W TH F S**

What did I do to grow in my relationship with God today?
- ○ Read the Bible   ○ Shared my faith
- ○ Prayed alone   ○ Prayed with a friend, family member, spouse
- ○ Served others   ○ Wrote in my prayer journal
- ○ Listened to Christian music

How did God bless me today? _____

_____

_____

_____

_____

What sins did I commit today? (List your confessions and seek forgiveness) _____

_____

_____

Who needs my prayers today? _____

_____

_____

_____

_____

_____

What did I learn today? _____

_____

_____

_____

What adjustments can I make in my life as a result of what I learned today? _____

_____

_____

_____

Daily reflections

TODAY IS: _____ **S M T W TH F S**

What did I do to grow in my relationship with God today?
- ○ Read the Bible   ○ Shared my faith
- ○ Prayed alone   ○ Prayed with a friend, family member, spouse
- ○ Served others   ○ Wrote in my prayer journal
- ○ Listened to Christian music

How did God bless me today? _____

_____

_____

_____

_____

What sins did I commit today? (List your confessions and seek forgiveness) _____

_____

_____

Who needs my prayers today? _____

_____

_____

_____

_____

What did I learn today? _____

_____

_____

_____

What adjustments can I make in my life as a result of what I learned today? _____

_____

_____

Prayers

Daily reflections

TODAY IS: _____   **S M T W TH F S**

What did I do to grow in my relationship with God today?
- ○ Read the Bible   ○ Shared my faith
- ○ Prayed alone   ○ Prayed with a friend, family member, spouse
- ○ Served others   ○ Wrote in my prayer journal
- ○ Listened to Christian music

How did God bless me today? _____

_____

_____

_____

_____

What sins did I commit today? (List your confessions and seek forgiveness) _____

_____

_____

Who needs my prayers today? _____

_____

_____

_____

_____

_____

What did I learn today? _____

_____

_____

_____

What adjustments can I make in my life as a result of what I learned today? _____

_____

_____

_____

Daily reflections

TODAY IS: _____ **S M T W TH F S**

What did I do to grow in my relationship with God today?

- ○ Read the Bible
- ○ Prayed alone
- ○ Served others
- ○ Listened to Christian music
- ○ Shared my faith
- ○ Prayed with a friend, family member, spouse
- ○ Wrote in my prayer journal

How did God bless me today? _____

_____

_____

_____

_____

What sins did I commit today? (List your confessions and seek forgiveness) _____

_____

_____

Who needs my prayers today? _____

_____

_____

_____

_____

_____

What did I learn today?_____

_____

_____

_____

What adjustments can I make in my life as a result of what I learned today?_____

_____

_____

_____

Prayers

Daily reflections

TODAY IS: _____   **S M T W TH F S**

What did I do to grow in my relationship with God today?

    ○ Read the Bible   ○ Shared my faith

    ○ Prayed alone   ○ Prayed with a friend, family member, spouse

    ○ Served others   ○ Wrote in my prayer journal

    ○ Listened to Christian music

How did God bless me today? _____

_____

_____

_____

_____

What sins did I commit today? (List your confessions and seek forgiveness) _____

_____

_____

Who needs my prayers today? _____

_____

_____

_____

_____

_____

What did I learn today? _____

_____

_____

_____

What adjustments can I make in my life as a result of what I learned today? _____

_____

_____

_____

Prayers

Daily reflections

TODAY IS: _____   **S M T W TH F S**

What did I do to grow in my relationship with God today?
- ○ Read the Bible
- ○ Prayed alone
- ○ Served others
- ○ Listened to Christian music
- ○ Shared my faith
- ○ Prayed with a friend, family member, spouse
- ○ Wrote in my prayer journal

How did God bless me today? _____

_____

_____

_____

_____

What sins did I commit today? (List your confessions and seek forgiveness) _____

_____

_____

Who needs my prayers today? _____

_____

_____

_____

_____

_____

What did I learn today? _____

_____

_____

_____

What adjustments can I make in my life as a result of what I learned today? _____

_____

_____

_____

Prayers

Daily reflections

TODAY IS: _____ **S M T W TH F S**

What did I do to grow in my relationship with God today?

◯ Read the Bible   ◯ Shared my faith

◯ Prayed alone   ◯ Prayed with a friend, family member, spouse

◯ Served others   ◯ Wrote in my prayer journal

◯ Listened to Christian music

How did God bless me today? _____

_____

_____

_____

_____

What sins did I commit today? (List your confessions and seek forgiveness) _____

_____

_____

Who needs my prayers today? _____

_____

_____

_____

_____

What did I learn today?_____

_____

_____

_____

What adjustments can I make in my life as a result of what I learned today?_____

_____

_____

Daily reflections

TODAY IS: _____ **S M T W TH F S**

What did I do to grow in my relationship with God today?
- ○ Read the Bible   ○ Shared my faith
- ○ Prayed alone   ○ Prayed with a friend, family member, spouse
- ○ Served others   ○ Wrote in my prayer journal
- ○ Listened to Christian music

How did God bless me today? _____

_____

_____

_____

_____

What sins did I commit today? (List your confessions and seek forgiveness) _____

_____

_____

Who needs my prayers today? _____

_____

_____

_____

_____

What did I learn today? _____

_____

_____

What adjustments can I make in my life as a result of what I learned today? _____

_____

_____

Prayers

Daily reflections

TODAY IS: _____   **S   M   T   W   TH   F   S**

What did I do to grow in my relationship with God today?
- ○ Read the Bible   ○ Shared my faith
- ○ Prayed alone   ○ Prayed with a friend, family member, spouse
- ○ Served others   ○ Wrote in my prayer journal
- ○ Listened to Christian music

How did God bless me today? _____

_____

_____

_____

_____

What sins did I commit today? (List your confessions and seek forgiveness) _____

_____

_____

Who needs my prayers today? _____

_____

_____

_____

_____

_____

What did I learn today?_____

_____

_____

_____

What adjustments can I make in my life as a result of what I learned today?_____

_____

_____

_____

Prayers

Daily reflections

TODAY IS: _____   **S M T W TH F S**

What did I do to grow in my relationship with God today?
- ○ Read the Bible
- ○ Prayed alone
- ○ Served others
- ○ Listened to Christian music
- ○ Shared my faith
- ○ Prayed with a friend, family member, spouse
- ○ Wrote in my prayer journal

How did God bless me today? _____

_____

_____

_____

_____

What sins did I commit today? (List your confessions and seek forgiveness) _____

_____

_____

Who needs my prayers today? _____

_____

_____

_____

_____

_____

What did I learn today? _____

_____

_____

_____

What adjustments can I make in my life as a result of what I learned today? _____

_____

_____

_____

Prayers

Daily reflections

TODAY IS: _____   **S M T W TH F S**

What did I do to grow in my relationship with God today?
- ○ Read the Bible
- ○ Prayed alone
- ○ Served others
- ○ Listened to Christian music
- ○ Shared my faith
- ○ Prayed with a friend, family member, spouse
- ○ Wrote in my prayer journal

How did God bless me today? _____

_____

_____

_____

_____

What sins did I commit today? (List your confessions and seek forgiveness) _____

_____

_____

Who needs my prayers today? _____

_____

_____

_____

_____

What did I learn today? _____

_____

_____

What adjustments can I make in my life as a result of what I learned today? _____

_____

_____

_____

Prayers

Daily reflections

TODAY IS: _____ **S M T W TH F S**

What did I do to grow in my relationship with God today?
- ○ Read the Bible
- ○ Prayed alone
- ○ Served others
- ○ Listened to Christian music
- ○ Shared my faith
- ○ Prayed with a friend, family member, spouse
- ○ Wrote in my prayer journal

How did God bless me today? _____

_____

_____

_____

_____

What sins did I commit today? (List your confessions and seek forgiveness) _____

_____

_____

Who needs my prayers today? _____

_____

_____

_____

_____

What did I learn today? _____

_____

_____

_____

What adjustments can I make in my life as a result of what I learned today? _____

_____

_____

_____

Daily reflections

TODAY IS: _____   **S M T W TH   F   S**

What did I do to grow in my relationship with God today?

- ○ Read the Bible   ○ Shared my faith
- ○ Prayed alone   ○ Prayed with a friend, family member, spouse
- ○ Served others   ○ Wrote in my prayer journal
- ○ Listened to Christian music

How did God bless me today? _____

_____

_____

_____

_____

What sins did I commit today? (List your confessions and seek forgiveness) _____

_____

_____

Who needs my prayers today? _____

_____

_____

_____

_____

_____

What did I learn today?_____

_____

_____

_____

What adjustments can I make in my life as a result of what I learned today?_____

_____

_____

_____

Prayers

Daily reflections

TODAY IS: _____   **S   M   T   W   TH   F   S**

What did I do to grow in my relationship with God today?
- ○ Read the Bible
- ○ Prayed alone
- ○ Served others
- ○ Listened to Christian music
- ○ Shared my faith
- ○ Prayed with a friend, family member, spouse
- ○ Wrote in my prayer journal

How did God bless me today? _____

_____

_____

_____

_____

What sins did I commit today? (List your confessions and seek forgiveness) _____

_____

_____

Who needs my prayers today? _____

_____

_____

_____

_____

What did I learn today?_____

_____

_____

What adjustments can I make in my life as a result of what I learned today?_____

_____

_____

Daily reflections

TODAY IS: _____   **S   M   T   W   TH   F   S**

What did I do to grow in my relationship with God today?
- ○ Read the Bible   ○ Shared my faith
- ○ Prayed alone   ○ Prayed with a friend, family member, spouse
- ○ Served others   ○ Wrote in my prayer journal
- ○ Listened to Christian music

How did God bless me today? _____

_____

_____

_____

_____

What sins did I commit today? (List your confessions and seek forgiveness) _____

_____

_____

Who needs my prayers today? _____

_____

_____

_____

_____

What did I learn today?_____

_____

_____

_____

What adjustments can I make in my life as a result of what I learned today?_____

_____

_____

_____

Prayers

Daily reflections

TODAY IS: _____   **S   M   T   W   TH   F   S**

What did I do to grow in my relationship with God today?
- ○ Read the Bible   ○ Shared my faith
- ○ Prayed alone   ○ Prayed with a friend, family member, spouse
- ○ Served others   ○ Wrote in my prayer journal
- ○ Listened to Christian music

How did God bless me today? _____

_____

_____

_____

_____

What sins did I commit today? (List your confessions and seek forgiveness) _____

_____

_____

Who needs my prayers today? _____

_____

_____

_____

_____

_____

What did I learn today? _____

_____

_____

_____

What adjustments can I make in my life as a result of what I learned today? _____

_____

_____

_____

Prayers

Daily reflections

TODAY IS: _____   **S M T W TH F S**

What did I do to grow in my relationship with God today?
- ○ Read the Bible   ○ Shared my faith
- ○ Prayed alone   ○ Prayed with a friend, family member, spouse
- ○ Served others   ○ Wrote in my prayer journal
- ○ Listened to Christian music

How did God bless me today? _____

_____

_____

_____

_____

What sins did I commit today? (List your confessions and seek forgiveness) _____

_____

_____

Who needs my prayers today? _____

_____

_____

_____

_____

_____

What did I learn today? _____

_____

_____

_____

What adjustments can I make in my life as a result of what I learned today? _____

_____

_____

_____

Prayers

Month in review

What specific actions did I take toward meeting my goals?

1. _____

2. _____

3. _____

What did I learn this month? (How did God guide me? How did he use me as an instrument to glorify him?)

_____

_____

_____

_____

_____

_____

_____

_____

_____

_____

_____

What adjustments can I make in my life as a result of what I learned this month?

_____

_____

_____

_____

_____

Notes

Customer Service Survey

If you enjoyed this journal, please help us by taking a few minutes to complete this survey. As a special "Thank You," we will send you news about new books, additional services, and upcoming special offers.

Please Print

Name _____

Address _____

_____

Fax number_____

E-mail _____Website _____

1. **What is your age?** ___18 or under ___19-25 ___26-39 ___40-49 ___50-60 ___60+

2. **What are your children's ages?** _____

3. **Marital Status:** ___married ___single ___divorced

4. **Was this book purchased by you?** ___yes ___no ___received as a gift

5. **How did you find out about this book?**
   ○ at a retreat   ○ at church   ○ personal recommendation
   ○ bookstore   ○ website   ○ mailing/e-mail   ○ other_____

6. **Please indicate your income level.**
   ○ Under $25,000   ○ $25,000-50,000   ○ $50,000-75,000
   ○ $75,000-100,000   ○ $100,000+

7. **Testimonial of how you have benefited from this journal** _____

_____

_____

_____

By sharing feedback directly from our customers, others are able to see how they can benefit from journaling. If you would like to share your testimonial, please sign below.

I grant Learning By Design permisson to use my testimonial for promotional purposes.

Name _____

Signature _____

Date _____

Thank you for your feedback. Please fax your reply to us at (612) 949-8738 or mail it to Learning By Design, P.O. Box 44926, Eden Prairie, MN 55344.

LEARNING By DESIGN — Custom Order Form

Product Code #	Product Description	Price
01	Prayer Journal for Busy Women	$14.95
02	Annual Supply: 4 total Prayer Journal for Busy Women	$51.80

SAVE $8!

Code No.	Qty.	GIFT (✔ Here)	Product	Price	Total

Subtotal	

SHIP TO: (PLEASE PRINT CLEARLY)

Name: _____

Address: _____

City: _____ State: _____

Zip: _____ Phone: _____

U.S. Shipping and Handling

1 Journal add $3.50	
4 Journals add $5.50	

Additional Shipping/Handling $3.50
(Per address — for each gift order)

Canadian Shipping $4.50

Other International Shipping $8.00
(Except Canada)

TOTAL

GIFT ORDERS SHIPPED TO:
SEE ADDITIONAL SHIPPING/HANDLING CHARGES IN ORDER FORM

Name: _____

Address: _____

City: _____ State: _____

Zip: _____ Quantity: _____

Name: _____

Address: _____

City: _____ State: _____

Zip: _____ Quantity: _____

Payment Method: (Please check one)

❑ Check/Money Order
Make checks payable to: Learning By Design

❑ VISA ❑ MasterCard

☐☐☐☐-☐☐☐☐-☐☐☐☐-☐☐☐☐
ACCOUNT NUMBER

Expiration Date: _____

Cardholder's Name: _____
PLEASE PRINT

Signature: _____

HOW TO ORDER:
Fax orders to: (612) 949-8738
Email orders to: salund@spacestar.com
Mail orders to: Susan Ayshe Lund
Learning By Design
P.O. Box 44926
Eden Prairie, MN 55346

 **Custom Order Form**

Product Code #	Product Description	Price
01	Prayer Journal for Busy Women	$14.95
02	Annual Supply: 4 total Prayer Journal for Busy Women	$51.80

SAVE $8!

Code No.	Qty.	GIFT (✔ Here)	Product	Price	Total

Subtotal

SHIP TO: (PLEASE PRINT CLEARLY)

Name: _____

Address: _____

City: _____ State: _____

Zip: _____ Phone: _____

U.S. Shipping and Handling

| 1 Journal add $3.50 |
| 4 Journals add $5.50 |

Additional Shipping/Handling $3.50
(Per address — for each gift order)

Canadian Shipping $4.50

Other International Shipping $8.00
(Except Canada)

TOTAL

Payment Method: (Please check one)

GIFT ORDERS SHIPPED TO:
SEE ADDITIONAL SHIPPING/HANDLING CHARGES IN ORDER FORM

Name: _____

Address: _____

City: _____ State: _____

Zip: _____ Quantity: _____

Name: _____

Address: _____

City: _____ State: _____

Zip: _____ Quantity: _____

❑ Check/Money Order
Make checks payable to: Learning By Design

❑ VISA ❑ MasterCard.

☐☐☐☐-☐☐☐☐-☐☐☐☐-☐☐☐☐

ACCOUNT NUMBER

Expiration Date: _____

Cardholder's Name: _____
PLEASE PRINT

Signature: _____

HOW TO ORDER:

Fax orders to: (612) 949-8738
Email orders to: salund@spacestar.com
Mail orders to: Susan Ayshe Lund
Learning By Design
P.O. Box 44926
Eden Prairie, MN 55346